BRIGHT
IDEA
BOOKS

CHADWICK
Boseman

by Aubrey Zalewski

CAPSTONE PRESS
a capstone imprint

Bright Idea Books are published by Capstone Press
1710 Roe Crest Drive, North Mankato, Minnesota 56003
www.mycapstone.com

Library of Congress Cataloging-in-Publication Data
Names: Zalewski, Aubrey, author.
Title: Chadwick Boseman / by Aubrey Zalewski.
Description: North Mankato, Minnesota : Capstone Press , [2020] | Series:
  Influential People. | Audience: Grades 4-6. | Includes index.
Identifiers: LCCN 2019003131 (print) | LCCN 2019007454 (ebook) | ISBN
  9781543571462 (ebook) | ISBN 9781543571332 (hardcover)
Subjects: LCSH: Boseman, Chadwick--Juvenile literature. | African American
  actors--Biography--Juvenile literature.
Classification: LCC PN2287.B645 (ebook) | LCC PN2287.B645 Z35 2020 (print) |
  DDC 791.4302/8092 [B] --dc23
LC record available at https://lccn.loc.gov/2019003131

All internet sites appearing in back matter were available and accurate when this book was sent
to press.

Editorial Credits
Editor: Claire Vanden Branden
Designer: Becky Daum
Production Specialist: Melissa Martin

Photo Credits
Alamy: D. Stevens/Universal Pictures/Photo 12, 18–19, Fox Studios/Entertainment Pictures,
14–15, Marvel Studios/Entertainment Pictures, 24–25; AP Images: Evan Agostini/Invision, cover;
Rex Features: Legendary Pictures/Kobal, 17, Michael Buckner/Variety, 21; Shutterstock Images:
Featureflash Photo Agency, 5, 28, 31, Kathy Hutchins, 9, 11, Pawika Tongtavee, 12–13, Sarunyu L,
6–7, Tinseltown, 23, 26–27

Design Elements: Shutterstock Images

Printed in the United States of America.
PA70

TABLE OF CONTENTS

CHAPTER 1

A REAL
Hero

The crowd cheered. Chadwick Boseman walked onto the stage. He put his hand to his chest. He took a deep breath. He had just won an award for Best Performance in a Movie.

Boseman won for playing King T'Challa in *Black Panther.* His character was the superhero Black Panther. It was the first Marvel movie with a mostly black **cast**. Boseman thanked the other actors in his speech. He said he could not have been a good hero without them.

Chadwick Boseman won Best Performance in a Movie at the 2018 MTV Movie & TV Awards.

Boseman is a hero in movies. But he also knows how to be one in real life. Boseman has visited sick children at St. Jude Children's Research Hospital. He spent time with the kids. They had a chance to meet a real superhero. Boseman wants to use his fame to help others.

Many kids look up to superheroes like Black Panther.

CHAPTER 2

FINDING
His Talents

Chadwick Boseman was born on November 29, 1977. He grew up in South Carolina.

Boseman enjoyed stories when he was little. His brother liked to dance and act. Boseman would watch him in plays. Boseman liked how plays told stories. But he did not want to act.

When Boseman was younger, he did not want to act in front of people. He grew to like acting as he got older.

Boseman played basketball in high school. One day Boseman's teammate was shot. He died. Boseman was very sad. He wrote a play to help with his feelings. He performed the play in his community. He realized he wanted to write and **direct**.

Boseman knew he wanted to work in the performing arts field.

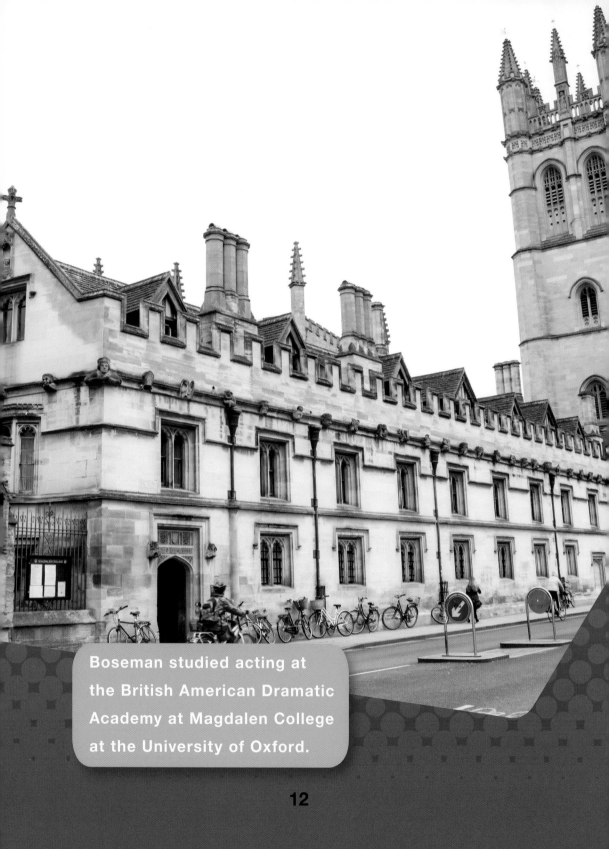

Boseman studied acting at the British American Dramatic Academy at Magdalen College at the University of Oxford.

COLLEGE YEARS

After high school Boseman went to Howard University. He studied directing. Boseman wanted to be a good director. So he had to learn how to act. He needed to know how actors worked. He needed to know how to talk to them. These **skills** would help him be a good director.

Boseman began to like acting. But he still wanted to direct.

Boseman stuck to his dream. He wrote plays. He did some directing. He also acted on TV shows. Soon Boseman would act in movies.

Boseman went from acting in small parts on television to having bigger parts in movies, like when he played Thoth in *Gods of Egypt* in 2016.

CHAPTER 3

SHARING
Important
Stories

In 2013 Boseman got his first big part. He starred in the movie *42*. He played Jackie Robinson. Robinson was a famous baseball player. He was the first black person to play baseball in the major leagues in the 20th century.

Boseman had to practice his baseball skills for the role of Jackie Robinson.

Boseman learned many kinds of dances when playing James Brown.

Boseman was in many movies after that. He played James Brown in *Get on Up* in 2014. Brown was a musician. He was a big part of black **culture**. He told black people to be proud.

In 2017 Boseman starred in *Marshall*. He played Thurgood Marshall. Marshall was the first black justice of the U.S. Supreme Court.

JAMES BROWN

Boseman had to play James Brown perfectly. He needed to dance and sing just like Brown. Many people loved Brown. Boseman was afraid he would get it wrong. He almost did not take the part. But he wanted the challenge.

Boseman has played important people. He wants to share their stories. Boseman thinks there should be more movies about black people. He has said many black stories have not been told. Others should know what black people have gone through.

Boseman is famous around the world.

CHAPTER 4

A DIFFERENT
Part

In 2018 Boseman's life changed forever. He starred in *Black Panther.* The movie showed parts of many different African cultures.

The movie was a huge hit. It was **nominated** for seven Academy Awards in 2019. These awards are given to the best movies in the world.

Boseman attended the 2019 Academy Awards, where *Black Panther* won three awards.

BLACK PANTHER

King T'Challa was a different part for Boseman. He was not playing a real person. But Boseman believes this part was just as important. The movie covered real problems in the world.

BIG SUCCESS

Black Panther broke many box office records. It made $242 million in its first weekend in theaters. It has made more than $1 billion across the world.

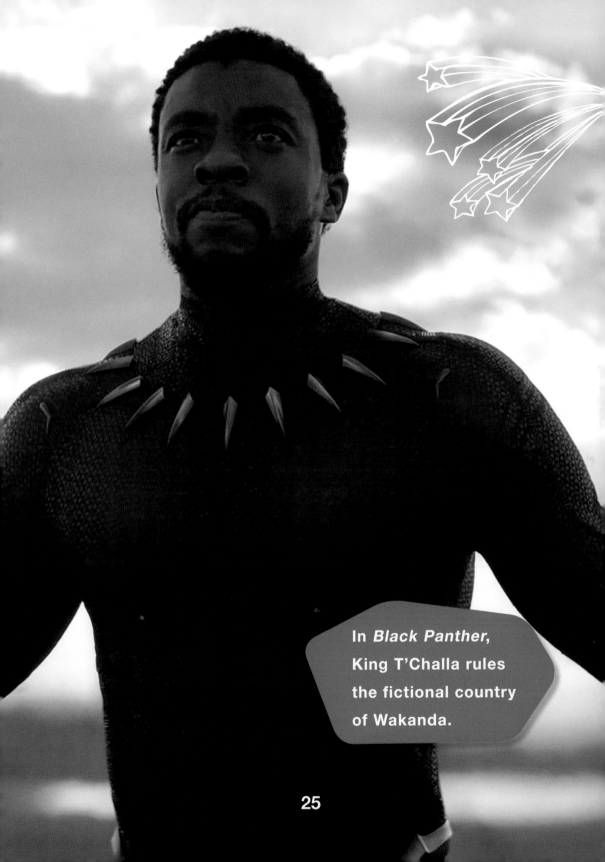

In *Black Panther*,
King T'Challa rules
the fictional country
of Wakanda.

Boseman wants to continue to take roles that tell black stories.

26

Black Panther was very popular around the world. Boseman wants to make movies with black characters more popular worldwide. *Black Panther* was a huge success. But Boseman says there is more work to be done.

GLOSSARY

cast
the people who have parts in a movie, play, or TV show

culture
the ideas and practices of a group of people

direct
to lead the actors and stage crew in a movie, play, or TV show

nominate
to suggest that a person might be the right one for a job or an award

skill
an ability to do something well

TIMELINE

1977: Chadwick Boseman is born in South Carolina.

2000: Boseman graduates from Howard University with a degree in directing.

2013: Boseman stars in the movie *42*.

2014: *Get on Up* is shown in theaters.

2017: Boseman stars as Thurgood Marshall in *Marshall*.

2018: Boseman stars in *Black Panther* as King T'Challa, the Black Panther.

ACTIVITY

WRITE AND DIRECT A PLAY

   Chadwick Boseman wrote plays before he acted. Try writing your own play. It can be based on your life, or it can be completely made up. Pick a topic that is important to you. After you have written your play, ask your friends to act it out. You can direct them or even act with them. Perform your play for an audience.

31

FURTHER RESOURCES

Want to know more about important people in black history? Take a look at these resources:

Heroes of Black History: Biographies of Four Great Americans. New York: Liberty Street, 2017.

PBS: Jackie Robinson
https://tpt.pbslearningmedia.org/resource/6a3f83c2-f961-4b22-8a54-e23a04dcc57b/jackie-robinson-video

Smith, Charles R., Jr. *28 Days: Moments in Black History that Changed the World*. New York: Roaring Brook Press, 2015.

Interested in learning about other black actors? Check out this resource:

Bell, Samantha S. *Jordan Peele*. Influential People. North Mankato, Minn.: Capstone Press, 2019.

INDEX